PRAYERS

PRAYERS

THEODORE
PARKER
FERRIS

THE SEABURY PRESS
NEW YORK

1981
The Seabury Press
815 Second Avenue
New York, N.Y. 10017

Printed in the United States of America

Library of Congress Cataloging in Publication Data

Ferris, Theodore Parker, 1908–1972
   Prayers.

   1. Prayers.   2. Prayer.   I.   Title.
BV245.F423   242'.8   80–26320
ISBN   0–8164–0483–6

CONTENTS

PART TWO

The Book of Prayer for Everyman by Theodore Parker Ferris, published in 1962, is out of print. It was, therefore, decided to produce a new book including not only the foreword About Prayer and most of the prayers from the former book but more than seventy additional prayers by Dr. Ferris.

ABOUT
PRAYER

The prayers in this book have been written over a period of
many years. As a matter of fact, most of them were not written but said at the end of a sermon. They were not premedi-
tated or carefully planned ahead of time, but were said spon-
taneously and freely when the sermon had come to its conclu-
sion. The prayer was the point toward which the sermon was
leading the people, and in it I tried to gather together our imperfect thoughts and lift them up where they might be used
by God in spite of their imperfection.

Some of the prayers, however, were written in the very be-
ginning. Among these are the hospital prayers, the daily
prayers, and the prayers that are obviously personal in their
purpose and content. I wrote them in my notebook with one
purpose only in mind — to help myself to pray. Like most
others who try to pray, my thoughts sometimes wander, my
desires are often confused and mixed up, and my mind is not
always clear. I found that when I wrote the prayers, my
thoughts could not wander so freely, my desires made themselves plainer, and there were some that I had not the face to
put on paper; and also that I could think more carefully than
when I rattled along in speech.

At the time, it never occurred to me that anyone else would

ever see these prayers that I had written in my notebook; and for years no one did. Then one of my dearest friends went to the hospital. The situation was serious. I wanted to help in every way I could and I ventured to give her the prayers I had written when I myself had been in the same hospital. By the grace of God they did help and since then I have not hesitated to give them to others in the hope that they too might find in them the words they were looking for.

It is in the same spirit that I now share them with a larger group. They will not speak for everyone, for we are all different, and we pray in different ways. Some of us are reserved in our prayers, while others have no reticence at all. Some are formal, some informal. Some prefer the familiar language of ancient prayers, and some are more at ease with the unfamiliar language of prayers that are still young.

It is always good when we can pray ourselves, in our own words, in our own peculiar style. But there are times when the words will not come, when the mind is weary, the body worn out, and the spirit limp. Then we turn gratefully to the words of some kindred spirit who can speak for us and take us into the Presence of the Most High where we can be still and know that he is God.

WHAT IS PRAYER?

It may be both appropriate and interesting to explore the question, What *is* prayer? It is almost impossible to say exactly what it is. Jesus himself never tried to do it. He said many things about prayer and he practiced it continually, but so far as we can tell from the Gospels, he never said what prayer really is.

I suppose it is something like trying to tell someone what music is if he has never heard it. Once he has heard it, you can discuss it with him, tell him a great many things about it — how it is made, what makes some of it good and some of it bad, how it should be played, and what it means. But until he has heard it, anything you say about it will mean little or nothing to him.

People who pray feel that they are in some kind of communication with God. They are either speaking to him or listening to him. What they say may be little more than a primitive cry for help. Or, it may be the promise to do God's will even though it mean their own death. It may be a word of gratitude when some unexpected brightness has come their way. It may be a word of regret after they have made some stupid mistake; or a more serious word of penitence when they know that they have not only made a mistake but committed a sin. It may be a word that expresses a longing for someone they love. More rarely, but more wonderfully, it may be a word of praise, a shout of gladness, for the glory overhead.

LISTENING TO GOD

Most people are more ready to speak to God than to listen to him speak to them. Some of them, well trained in other ways, have never understood what it means to say that God speaks to people. They have never heard God speak, never heard anything that they could recognize as the Divine Voice, and because they have not themselves heard God speak they assume that he never speaks. They have never stopped to think that language is only one of many means of communication, and not always the most effective one.

A great painting speaks to you without ever a word being uttered. A situation speaks to you, calls to you, demands something of you, without a word being said. And there comes a point when two people who are in love become silent because there are no words to say what they are saying to each other without any words at all.

God speaks to you in a language all his own, and it is not

always the same language. Sometimes it is the language of conscience, and the voice is the stern voice of duty. Sometimes he speaks in the language of beauty, the most visual of all his languages, but lost on many an eye that has been blinded by vulgarity and ugliness. To some who are able to understand he speaks in the language of suffering, the most universal of all languages, the most easily misunderstood, and the one capable of saying things that none of the others can say.

One thing is certain. No matter how God may choose to speak to you, you will not hear him unless you listen, and you cannot listen until you yourself are still. You must learn to sit still, learn to be still, like the waters of a lake, which on a windless day reflect a perfect image of what is around and above them. This is perhaps one of the hardest things in the world for a modern American to do. The very idea of it is strange to him who has been brought up on the idea that there is something sacred about activity, some inherent virtue in being busy. He will go to committee meetings all day long and feel that he is doing something good, even though most of the meetings accomplish little or nothing. But the thought of being still for half an hour so that he might hear what God is saying to him strikes him as an utter waste of his precious time.

Even when he wants to do it, he finds it difficult. To find the time and place is not easy; to stop the wheels of the machinery is a hard thing to do. Prayer was never easy, not even in the first century Galilee. It is as natural for a man to pray as it is for him to shout, but there is a long, long way between that instinctive shout and the prayer in the Garden of Gethsemane. The distance between the two is never covered without real effort and without a considerable amount of anguish.

Those who make the effort reap the harvest; those who give up miss the opportunity of being in some sort of conscious communication with the Source of all being, who is beyond us and yet within us, drawing us toward a fuller and richer life, waiting for us to show some sign that we are waiting and watching for him.

HOW JESUS PRAYED

Prayer, then, is a means of communication between you and God. There will be times, I fear, when you will wonder whether there is a God, and if there is, whether you can be in any real communication with him. This, of course, is the biggest question that anyone can ask, and I could not answer it adequately if I had all the time and space that I needed. I shall point, therefore, to one fact upon which I stand when questions like this one begin to unsettle me. The fact is that Jesus prayed.

One of the things we know about Jesus beyond the shadow of a doubt is that he prayed. When the heavens opened at his baptism, and that one clear call of God came to him, what was he doing? He was praying. The night before he chose the twelve men who were to be most intimately associated with him in his incomparable task, what was he doing? He spent the whole night in prayer. After a strenuous day of healing and working with the crowds and the multitudes that were pressing in upon him from every side, what did he do? He withdrew himself into the wilderness and prayed.

Before he asked the disciples the question, Who do people think I am? — the crucial question, the question that was to be the watershed of religious history — what was he doing? He was praying. When he was transfigured on the mountain top, when the fashion of his countenance was altered and his raiment became white and glistering, what was he doing? The account in the Gospel says, "While he was praying the whole appearance of his face changed." The night before he died, where was he? In a garden, praying. When the end came and he was nailed to a tree, what was he doing? Praying, first for his executioners and then for himself.

The unmistakable impression that the Gospel leaves is that Jesus and prayer are inseparable. Think of the life of Jesus as a fine tapestry. If you try to pull out the golden threads of prayer, the whole fabric falls apart.

We turn, therefore, wistfully to Jesus. If you are drawn at all to him, he will draw you into prayer. If you are not drawn at all, of course he will not. But if you are drawn at all to him, he will draw you into prayer just as he once did, and in the same way—not by telling you that you must do it, but by doing it himself. You will begin to say to yourself, as I have said so many times when I have struggled with my own doubts, He knew too much to be deceived. He may not have known all the laws that govern outer space, he may not have known how the universe operates scientifically, but he knew things more important than these things, and he knew too much to be deceived. I cannot imagine that in those long nights when he was alone with his Father he was utterly deceived. I cannot believe it. Anything that occupied as much of his time as prayer did must have something more than some of us see in it, and cannot be beneath the consideration of any person, no matter how much he knows or how highly educated he may be.

What Jesus Teaches Us About Prayer

Also, he never tells us exactly what prayer is. He starts now as he did then with what we have. It may be only a cry in the night. Then he begins to train and deepen that primitve cry. I knew a portrait painter once who was engaged to paint a portrait of a person that he had not seen for eighteen years. He thought he knew the person but during the eighteen years the person had changed, and when the sitter went for the first sitting, the painter looked at him and said, "I've got to get a bigger canvas." It wasn't that he couldn't get the person on the canvas that he had prepared; it was that there were moral and spiritual proportions in the person that a canvas of the original size could not possibly suggest.

I keep hearing Jesus say to me, You have got to get a bigger canvas for your prayer; it has got to be bigger than your little needs, important as they are, cries in the night. It has got to be a canvas great enough for the grandeur of God, and his will and his purpose; and until you get that larger canvas, prayer will mean nothing to you. If you persist in thinking of a God sitting above the heavens ready to pull strings here and there to make things come out right for you and for those you love, your prayer will gradually wither away.

And finally, he will almost surely lead us away from the crowd into some quiet place. He slipped away into the wilderness. He went up onto the mountain apart, alone, to pray. In some ways there is nothing like public prayer as it takes place in a church building. But this is no substitute for solitude. You will never find what Jesus meant by prayer until you are alone with God.

Then you say to yourself, Where in the world can I find such a place? If you are young you say, My house is in a constant turmoil, with children, and dishes, and everything that has to be done. And the city has its noise and confusion and dirt and distraction — where can I find such a place? I can tell you. A church — any church.

I have never been one to desire to begin movements, but if there is one movement I should like to begin this is it — and I know how difficult it would be. I should like to begin a movement in which the members would promise, when possible, to spend twenty minutes a day in a church, some church, somewhere. At first they might not know what to do, and I would not mind that. They could just sit still, and let the currents of God sweep over them until they began to feel them, and the time would come when they would know what to say. You say twenty minutes is too long; nobody can afford that amount of time. Ten minutes is too little. It is better than nothing, but you cannot get really unwound in ten minutes. You have to sit long enough to do it. To drop on your knees and say a prayer and dash out is better than nothing, but it is not what Jesus meant by prayer.

A good modern theologian who confesses his ineptness in prayer goes on to say, "All we know is that somehow our style of life must make room in our world of noise and movement for the silence, the waiting, the withdrawal of the life of prayer." How well we know that! Knowing that, we look to Jesus and we say, Lord Jesus, take us apart from the world; teach us to pray; show us the Father.

Help us, Lord, to be master of ourselves
That we may become the servants of others.
Take our lips and speak through them
Our minds and think through them
And take our hearts and set them on fire.
                                    Amen

PART ·I·

DAILY PRAYERS

THE LORD'S PRAYER

Our Father, who art in heaven, Hallowed be thy Name. Thy kingdom come. Thy will be done, On earth as it is in heaven. Give us this day our daily bread. And forgive us our trespasses, As we forgive those who trespass against us. And lead us not into temptation, But deliver us from evil. For thine is the kingdom, and the power, and the glory, for ever and ever. Amen.

In the Morning:

I thank thee, O God, for the day which thou hast made. I will rejoice and be glad in it. Whether it be bright or dark, I will accept it without fear or complaint. Whatever it brings, I will try to meet it as well as I can. And knowing that all things work together for good to them that love thee, I shall go about my work in quietness and in confidence. Tomorrow I cannot see, but today is mine because it is thine.

At Noontime:

O God, who hast taught us to come apart from the world and rest awhile, help us to set aside all our cares and concerns that we may look only upon the brightness of thy Being, and think only of thy power and love. Ease the tensions of our bodies and set our minds at rest, that we may be ready to receive that which thou art so ready to give. Help us to lose ourselves in the wonder of thy presence that we may find ourselves renewed to do thy will.

In the Evening:

We pause at the ending of the day to thank thee, O God, for life itself; for the wonders of existence, for our family and friends; our food and shelter and all the necessities of life; we thank thee, also, for all the unexpected things that make life happy and bright, and for the common things, like water and light; we are grateful too for all the difficulties of life, the sorrows and hardships, for by them and through them we enter more and more deeply into the meaning of existence.

For Others:

O God, the Maker and Father of us all, we bring into the light of thy presence those who need thy care and help, especially those whom we love; make them sure of thy presence and power, and so open their minds and hearts to thyself that thou canst give them the things which thou hast prepared for those who love thee; take away their fears and renew their spirits day by day.

For Myself:

Whenever I am downcast, O Lord, help me to remember the people I have enjoyed and loved. I hope I neither forget them when they are gone, nor take them for granted while they are alive. Those who have meant so much to me, may I mean increasingly more to them. Bind us together, O Lord, in such a way that our lives may share the glory and the pain that comes to each of us, and grant that as I walk in the strength of the ones who are stronger than I, I may also suffer for the sake of the ones who are weaker than I.

———

O God, when I think of thee I forget my aches and pains. Fill my mind with cares and concerns so great that they will crowd out my little complaints. Help me to accept my physical limitations and take them without wishing I were made in a different way. Thou hast made me as I am, and I have not always done the best I could with what I have. Let me always remember, and never forget, how many times I have come through. If I must miss things that other people seem to enjoy, help me to let those things go, without losing either my gladness or my love.

———

Teach me, O Lord, not to hold on to life too tightly. Teach me to hold it lightly; not carelessly, but lightly, easily. Teach me to take it as a gift, to enjoy and to cherish while I have it, and to let it go gracefully and thankfully when the time comes. The gift is great, but the Giver is greater still. Thou, O God, art the Giver and in thee is the Life that never dies.

THE
CHRISTIAN
YEAR

ADVENT

O God, we thank thee for the coming of thy Son Jesus Christ
into our world and into our lives. He comes as a gift for which
we are joyfully thankful. Help us to prepare ourselves for that
second coming when he comes looking for the fruits of the
Spirit. We ask this in the name of Jesus, our Lord, our Judge
and our Friend.

―――――――

Let us be still, and remember Jesus as he was then, powerful
to heal, to speak, to save. Think of him as he is now, powerful
as the Spirit of God among us, to lift us up out of the low
places and set our feet once again on the high way. O God,
draw us to him who is the perfect incarnation of thyself, that
our power may more and more be tamed by the power of his
love.

―――――――

O God, may we simplify our lives that we be not so concerned
with unimportant things that we miss the real thing. Open

7

our eyes to him who is already among us, and who will come again into our midst on Christmas, that we may see his brightness, even in the dim surroundings, and recognize his greatness even in his weakness. Give us this second sight, O God, that our lives may be saved from meaninglessness and sin.

————

Sharpen our minds, O Lord; humble our spirits, and open our hearts to take in the love that once became flesh, that comes amongst us again and again, that we may not only take him in, but show him to others and let others see him in us. And we ask it in his name, and by his power, and for his sake.

————

O God, who hast put a restlessness in our hearts and a thirst for thee in our very nature, turn us now in the right direction. Give us the grace to realize that there are no easy answers to our questions and no shortcuts to our goal. As we move toward Christmas, help us to search our own hearts and look at the life of the church and ask if there be any evil way in it, so that we may be ready to receive the new life that is coming.

CHRISTMAS

We thank thee, O God, for the light that came into our world in the life of Jesus. Help us as we try to catch that light in our own lives; let it shine through us to pierce the darkness of some dark place this Christmas. We ask these things in the name of him who was born in a stable, Jesus Christ our Lord. As we try to find our way through the dangerous places in life, through the dark tunnels of everyday existence, open our eyes, O God, to see thee as thou didst come to us in Jesus. Give us the grace to trust him and to find in him all thy power and love, the fullness of thy very Being, so that knowing that thou dost love us, we can love thee and all our neighbors in response. We ask this as we remember how thou camest to us a tiny baby thing that made a woman cry.

––––––––––

We thank thee, O God, for the light that shines in the darkness, for the Christ who came into our world, and who uses us to be instruments of his glory and love. As we rejoice at Christmas, without forgetting the sadness and the sorrow that is all abroad in the world, we remember that light which the darkness cannot put out and which, if we will let it, will shine in us.

––––––––––

Lord, show us the way of light and love. We know what we ought to do. Teach us how to do it.

––––––––––

By way of Bethlehem lead us, O Lord, to
    newness of life;
by the innocence of the Christ Child renew
    our simple trust;
by the tenderness of Mary deliver us from
    cruelty and hardness of heart;
by the patience of Joseph save us from all
    rash judgment and ill-tempered action;
by the shepherds' watch open our eyes to
    the signs of thy coming;
by the wise men's journey keep our search-
    ing spirits from fainting;
by the music of the heavenly choir put to
    shame the clamor of the earth;
by the shining of a star guide our feet into
    the way of peace.

––––––––––

O God, as we try to find our way through the world we live in, help us to remember how into our imperfect world thou didst

9

once come, simply and quietly, and how the spirit of Christ comes again and again to us, and through us to other people to save their lives from drudgery and fear, sickness and sin. O God, let this life be in us this Christmas tide, that in lives that otherwise might be dark there may be glory and peace.

————

Set a star, O Lord, in the night sky to
    lighten our darkness and to guide our feet into the
    way of peace;
Take flesh and blood once more upon thyself that love
    may dwell among us;
Reveal thyself, O Mighty God, in small and tender things
    that we be not deceived or dismayed by things that
    tower above us;
Show forth, O Father of Life, the beauty of motherhood
    that our families may be clothed with sanctity;
Speak again, O God, from the lips of a child that our
    wordly wisdom may be chastened;
Send thy Son among us, O thou Lord of Life, that he
    may renew our flagging spirits and save us from disas-
    ter and the dark.

————

O God, as we remember the visit thou didst once make to this wayside planet, open our eyes that we may see thy presence everywhere. Quicken our minds that we may think more alertly and acutely about the places in the world where we can serve most usefully, and open our hearts that thou mayest come into our lives and make them new. Then use us in the ministry of thy Son, Jesus Christ, to tell other people about thy visit.

————

May the joy of Christmas fill your days with gladness;
May the peace of Christmas take away your anxious care;

10

May the light of Christmas shine through your deepest
    darkness;
And may the love of him who was born on
    Christmas day go with you in all your ways.

———————

Lord Jesus, come into our world and heal its wounds;
        Come into our homes and make them holy;
        Come into our work and make it fruitful;
        Come into thy Church and save it from falling;
        Come into our minds and keep them clear;
        Come into our lives and make them good;
Come quickly, Lord Jesus.

———————

As the Christmas season passes once again, O God, may the
light of it linger in our lives, so that we see the whole world in
a new way and from a new point of view. Give us the grace
and the will to trust the best in other people and to look constantly for thee, not in the sky but in our own lives.

THE NEW YEAR

Grant, O Lord, that we go fearlessly into the New Year with
our eyes open, our hearts pure, and our hands ready to serve
and to minister to those who need us. Help us to be where the
need is greatest, and save us from all narrowness and preju-
dice. And above all take us out of the past and put us into the
lively climate of the present.

———————

O God, our Father and Creator, as we embark upon the difficult and hazardous ways of the years that lie ahead, give us the
will to live, gladly, confidently, and the grace to accept and take
anything that comes to us, knowing that thou art about our
ways guiding us, sustaining us, helping us to reach the goal.

11

EPIPHANY

We bring to thee, O God, the best we have and offer it to him who is the Light of the World, for we recognize in him that which makes manifest the hidden things of darkness. Help us to show forth in our own lives such a measure of that Life that other people may be drawn out of the shadows into the brightness and glory of it.

―――――――

Open our minds, O God, to the thoughts of thee and of thy purpose for us. Grant that we may never settle down in the familiar and the comfortable, so that we are not ready to rise up and follow the stars that lead us on and on. Help us in our life here on earth to start out on the great adventure of finding a way of life with our fellow men and women as we have been taught by our Lord and Saviour, Jesus Christ.

―――――――

Ye have heard it said . . . but I say . . .

O God, help us to show forth the light and spirit of Jesus in our own lives by being more like him in our action and in our behavior; and as we try to rise above our own natural, animal existence, give us the grace that we need to achieve, at least at rare moments, the unattainable.

ASH WEDNESDAY

Guide us, O God, as we try to follow Jesus into the wilderness; take away all sham and hypocrisy and help us to make this season a period of growth in our own understanding of ourselves and in our usefulness to others; keep us close to him as we try to follow him from the wilderness into the woods, and out to the hill and finally into the skies. We ask this in the name of Jesus our Lord and Master.

12

And he was there in the wilderness forty days tempted of Satan.

O Lord Christ, as thou didst face grave questions about the mission that God called thee to do, so we face questions about our purpose in life. Grant that we may always remember thee, how when thou wast tempted to do something good, but not good enough, thou didst stand firm, and setting aside all compromise and all play for popularity, thou didst set thy face toward Jerusalem, like a flint. Be with us in our time of testing, O thou tempted One who did not sin.

LENT

Help us, O God, as we draw apart from the world during this season of refreshment and renewal, to see Jesus with new eyes and understanding, and to find in him that which makes him unlike all others who ever lived. Help us when we see him to follow him and to show him to the world we live in; all these things we ask in his name.

———————

O God, as we stand and look at the figure of Jesus, trying to enter into closer association with him, and as we watch the wave of his popularity gradually receding until there is not one soul left, help us in our feebleness to stand loyal to him who we know is the Truth and the Way and the Life. We ask this knowing that he will help us; he will understand our failures and make allowance for our weakness.

———————

O God, we thank thee from the bottom of our hearts for the life that was in Jesus; help us as these days move on toward Good Friday and Easter to understand more clearly and to appreciate more completely what that life really is like until finally we may kneel before him and adore him and let his life lift our lives up to be with him.

13

. . . he hath showed thee, O man, what is good . . .

O God, as we try sincerely to follow the directions that come from thee so that our lives may be lived creatively and usefully, help us to keep our eyes fixed upon thee as the great Conductor of life, and to follow any directions that may come from thee. But when there are no directions, help us to read the music as it is written, and to hear it as it was played by Jesus of Nazareth, that we may catch in our own lives an echo of the strains of his music.

PALM SUNDAY

Help us, O God, as we try to follow Jesus through the crowded ways of the city into the Temple and then out to the Mount of Olives. Open our minds as we hear him answering questions; set our hearts free to feel for him and with him as he goes to his death; and above all, give us the will to put our trust in him and pledge our loyalty to him, that in spite of all the doubts that beset us and all the evidence of darkness and evil, we may follow steadily in his train, on to the cross, and to life.

We thank thee, O God, for the knowledge and vision of Jesus, our Lord and Master, as he went quietly into the Holy City on this day; help us so to follow in his steps, more ready to serve than to be served, that we may lose our lives and find them in him. We ask this in recognition of all our divided loyalties. O God, accept our praises and hosannas in the spirit in which we offer them, and pardon our offenses.

As we try to follow our Lord and Master into the city where he was hailed as a king, help us, O God, to show forth in our lives something of his incomparable spirit, that people seeing us may be renewed in confidence and courage and know that once again thou hast triumphed.

14

Maundy Thursday
Holy Communion

May the bread and wine open our eyes, O God, to the presence of Christ among us. Bind us more closely to each other and to him and lift up our hearts and minds to thee, that we may go out renewed in body and soul, fed, nourished, made new.

So they drew near to the village to which they were going. He appeared to be going further, but they constrained him, saying, Stay with us, for it is toward evening, and the day is now far spent.

Help us, O God, to see through the veils of material things to the presence of our Lord Christ in this meal, so that we who sometimes are weary and worn by our striving after that which is unattainable may be rested and renewed by him who comes amongst us to tarry with us, Jesus our Lord and Master.

Lead us, O Lord, ever more deeply into the mysteries of life and death as we see them revealed in the bread and wine of the Last Supper of thy Son Jesus Christ. May we see there plainly, clearly and simply stated, the meaning of our existence and of thy purpose for us and all thy people everywhere. We ask this in the name of Jesus who died that we might live.

Good Friday

God forbid that I should glory, save in the cross of our Lord Jesus Christ.

In thy cross, O Christ, we glory.
In thy pain we see our shame,

In thy love we find our hope.
  Break through our hard and heartless
    ways with the sight of perfect good-
    ness put to death;
  Bring us back to our senses, Lord,
  And show us how the suffering leads to
    glory,
  And how the glory covers all our pain.

EASTER

We thank thee, O God, for the life and death of Jesus, his presence with us now; help us to see him more clearly, to love him more dearly and to follow him more nearly, that his risen life may be in us; and as we die to the little things of the world, may we live with him in light and love and life.

––––––––

O God, we thank thee for the life and the death and the risen Jesus, opening as it does to us the larger areas of life. Help us to make the most of them, not to be satisfied with the shallows of cynical and doubting and skeptical minds; take our natural impulses, O God, and stretch them; confirm them and reassure them on this day of resurrection, in the name of him who though his body was destroyed yet is now present among us.

––––––––

And very early in the morning, the first day of the week, they came unto the sepulchre at the rising of the sun.

We thank thee, O God, for the life of Jesus and for the love that was revealed and released by his death. Help us so to share in the quality of his life that we may share in the triumph of his victory. We ask this in the name of him who told us, "Because I live, ye shall live also."

16

Lift us, O God, from the lower levels of life up into those higher regions where our spirits can grow to their full stature. Give us the new life that is in Christ and help us to give it to other people who are waiting to be raised from the dead.

We thank thee, O God, for life with all its wonder and beauty and power, and especially for the life of Jesus as we see him revealed on a day like this, when the limitations of time and space are set aside and he goes forward to his life among us as love and power and wisdom. Help us, O God, so to order our lives that the weight of our interest may be on the side of eternal things, and when it comes time to gather us together unto our fathers, we shall know whither we are going. We ask these things in the name of Jesus who on this day was raised from the dead.

Let the life that was in Christ Jesus, O God, be in us, and let it be radiated from us and through us to other people. Give us the power and the grace to go out into our world and live as though Christ were living in us, that our world may be raised from death to life.

Rogation Sunday

O God, who art the source of every good thing in our lives, when we pray help us to remember that all we have or ever hope to be comes from thee. And then give us the grace to ask for the things that we want most, leaving it to thy judgment and thy goodness to grant them or to withhold them. Teach us, Lord Jesus, in this hard world of mechanism and impersonal enterprise to pray, and to pray wisely and humbly.

Ascension

Open our eyes, O God, to the heavenly splendors of Christ and open our mind and understanding that we may see through the pictures and the language of our faith to its real meaning and significance; then as we move through the troubled ways of life, may the heaven in which he now dwells be all around and about us, and may the lives which we now live be lifted up to heights unknown.

———

I am with you always, even unto the end of the world.

O God who hast given us so many good and wonderful things that sometimes seem to be snatched so cruelly away from us, help us to learn as we think of the Ascension of Jesus that while the good things of life seem to be taken away, nevertheless, in their going sometimes we find our good; and that above and beyond the coming and going of life there is a realm in which all good things continually are. For these things we are thankful, O God.

Pentecost
Whitsunday

We thank thee, O God, for thy church and we ask that thou wilt make us more useful servants of it; help us within the context of this fellowship to accept ourselves, to love our neighbor, and to trust thy power and love. We ask these things, O Lord, in the midst of all our trials and tribulations, knowing that wherever two or three are gathered together in thy name, thou art there.

———

Give my love to the little church that meets in their house.

We thank thee, O God, for the church that has met in various places down through the ages, sometimes in great cathedrals

18

and sometimes in catacombs and sometimes in the fields. Help us to recover in our own lives the thing that makes the church its real self, and then send us out to carry that spirit of the living Christ into our homes, our offices, our schools, wherever we may be.

We thank thee, O God, for thy church in which all faithful people are gathered together in all lands. May it never be complacent. May its doors never be closed. May its heart and mind always be open to those who make any sign of movement for itself. We ask this in the spirit of Jesus, whose spirit came to us on Pentecost.

We are thankful, O God, for the church which has continued the ministry of Jesus through the ages and committed it to our care and trust. Imperfect though we be, help us to dedicate ourselves so completely to this ministry that we may go out into the world not to condemn it but to save it, and to reclaim it for a life that is good and true and beautiful.

Gather us together, O God, in the fellowship of thy faithful people. May we never forget what the church has done for our world and for us. Keep us ever mindful of the fact that we are the church, and that if we cease to grow, if we stand stiff in our pride, if we let the flames die, the church dies with us. Pardon our failures, O God, and give us the will and the power to continue the ministry of Jesus in the world of the future.

TRINITY SUNDAY

The grace of the Lord Jesus Christ, and the love of God, and the fellowship of the Holy Spirit, be with you all.

Open the eyes of our understanding, O God, that we may perceive the mysteries of thy truth; keep us simple as we try to work out our own way of life, and yet grant that we do not miss the deeps of life. Help us to remember, always, that thy goodness and thy power and thy presence with us are always one and the same; that thou art three persons, ever inseparably united in one majestic, transcendent God.

ALL SAINTS

We thank thee, O God, for those whose names shine like stars in the dark firmament. When we are discouraged, remind us of the race they once ran and give us the will to follow in their train, knowing that the race is worth the running and that it runs out into light and joy and fellowship with thee.

O God, open our eyes that we may see those who are invisible, and lift us up above the fogs of life. Lead us out into the larger spaces where men dare to believe things they cannot prove. As the years carry us along, and we ourselves approach the veil of the invisible, so increase our faith and sharpen our vision that we may see more and more clearly those who are invisible.

For all those who reach upward toward the shores of light, we give thee thanks, O God. May they shine in our darkness to give us courage and faith, and as we go about our own way, may we follow their example and reach out more and more to the things that are beyond our immediate grasp, through Jesus Christ our Lord.

Look, the heavens are opened, and I can see the Son of man standing on the right hand of God.

We thank thee, O God, for the lives of thy chosen ones in whom there has been grace and power; draw us more closely into their fellowship that by association with them our lives may be quickened, and that we may be encouraged to strike out into the deeps of our own lives and live them with as much honesty and courage as they lived theirs.

O God, we thank thee for the lives through which the light of thy presence has come into our world. Help us to learn from them as we know them more and more; and as we are drawn to Jesus our Lord and Master, grant that we may be grafted into him, rooted in him, so that our lives may be his instrument, and that he may be in us and we in him.

Thanksgiving Day

O God, we thank thee for life, and all the beauty and the wonder of it, for the people that we have known and loved, and for the rare opportunities that we have had to enter into the deeper things of life; forgive, O God, our triviality, and overlook our foolish ways. Help us to deepen and cultivate our understanding of primary things, things that come first, and then give us the will and the grace to make this nation strong that it may endure and that it may not go the way of others into exile and oblivion.

O God, we thank Thee for the bounty of our land. Save us from taking it for granted, and spare us from softness of spirit and hardness of heart.

PRAYERS
TO FATHER, SON,
AND HOLY SPIRIT

GOD: HIS WORD AND PRESENCE

The Lord is King, be the people never so impatient.

The Lord God omnipotent reigneth.

*Thine is the kingdom, O Lord, and thou art exalted
   as head above all.*

We see in our lives, O God, the signs of thy ruling. Help us to
temper our wills accordingly, and grant that as we go about
our business we may say to ourselves, Thy will be done, not
ours, in the assurance that in life and in death, in normal times
and in hard times, thou art ruling over all things for our good,
and for the good of the world, and that in thy good time thou
wilt bring all things to the fulfillment of thy purpose.

O God, we thank thee for the story of deliverance and eman-
cipation. When we are trapped in the entanglements of life
that almost threaten our very existence, help us to remember

what happened at the Red Sea when thou didst rule and make thy rule known, when the waters were turned back and men walked through on dry land.

———————

Open our minds, O God, and our spirits to the beauty and the truth of thy word that it may light our path and ease our burden; and direct us through the difficult and dangerous ways of our lives.

———————

O thou invisible God, whom we cannot see and yet whom we know, help us to see the reflection of thy goodness and power in the things that thou hast made. Give us the will and the mind to read thy messages that have been preserved for us in the Bible, and hold before us continually the picture of thy everlasting love in the face of Jesus Christ. Give us the grace in the midst of the confusion and disquietude of this world to stop from time to time whatever we are doing to think about thee.

———————

. . . and Jacob was left alone; and there wrestled a man with him until the breaking of the day.

O God, the determiner of our destiny, how often we try to escape thy presence and thy judgment; and yet, how inevitably we are ultimately brought to that place where we meet thee face to face in the lonely struggles of the night. Help us to take the wounds that are inflicted upon us and use them for thy glory and for our good. We ask this in the name of Jesus our Lord.

———————

Surely the Lord is in this place, and I knew it not.

O God, thou art in every place, and thy presence is all about us. Help us not to be so pressed by the concerns and cir-

24

cumstances of our daily lives that we lose the consciousness of thy presence, for by it we will climb the ladder from earth to heaven.

———

We know, O God, that everything we are and have, and everything that we can ever hope to be, ultimately comes from thee. Keep alive in us that sense of dependence upon thee, and give us the grace and the wisdom so to co-operate with thy laws, that we may work together with thee to do things which by ourselves we could never accomplish at all.

———

O God, who didst make all things, and who hast given to us the gift and wonder of life, help us to walk softly through thy world, obeying its laws, respecting its wonders, and give us also that confidence which comes from knowing that all things can be remade by thy power and love.

———

We have this treasure in earthen vessels.

O God, who hast shown us the light of thy life and love in Jesus, and hast filled our hearts with a sense of thy nearness and presence, and given our lives new meaning and significance as we are drawn closer to thee in the vast universe of life, grant that the light that we have seen may shine in us to make another life bright, and to give the assurance to someone who needs it that thou art, and that thou dost care.

———

For thine inescapable presence, O God, we give thee thanks, for without thy probing finger we would grow so dull and dead to what is right and wrong that our lives would be completely lost. Confront us with the things that are eternally good, and draw us ever toward them by him who is like the magnet of the pole, even Jesus Christ our Lord.

O God, who art the source of all strength and power, help us to preserve a real sense of our own dignity, and at the same time help us to remember that in ourselves and of ourselves we can do nothing. Help us to understand more fully and trust more completely the power that thou didst show in Jesus, the power of pure, unqualified goodness, and then give us courage to trust in that power, come what will, knowing that when we have used our strength thou wilt add unto it all of thine.

———————

Open the eyes and ears of our understanding, O God, to thy presence that we may enter into the fullness of life as creatures of thine, destined to some purpose, great or small, in the world. Send us out from this place sobered by the thought of thee and encouraged by the knowledge that thou art ever by our side, to help us and to give us the strength to do the things that thou hast asked us to do.

———————

Stir up in us, O God, that divine discontent with the inner attitudes of our lives. Help us to examine them honestly and then come thou into our hearts and minds like light and love to which we may offer everything that we are and have. We ask this in the name of Jesus.

———————

O God, who hast given us eyes to see and ears to hear, and fingers to touch, we thank thee for all the signs of thy presence. Help us from time to time to separate ourselves from all outward things and in the empty room be aware of a Presence greater than anything could ever represent, the Being which is the ground of our existence, and the Love that moves us, and the sun and all the other stars.

———————

O God, whom we cannot see, draw us into thyself, into thy presence, that we may go out strengthened, renewed, full of confidence that we can meet whatever comes to us, reassured and joyful, knowing that in spite of all the difficulties, life makes sense; and that life is good in spite of all its pain.

JESUS: HIS GRACE AND DISCIPLESHIP

Do violence to no man.

O God, who hast revealed in Jesus a new spiritual power which can heal broken relationships and overcome even the most stalwart enemies, open our eyes that we may know and understand him, and stir our hearts that we may admire him as we try to work out in the troubled world of our time the whole question of violence. We ask this, O God, in all humility, knowing the limitation and inadequacy of our thinking and the weakness of our wills.

———

Let us be still in the presence of him who is the way, the truth, and the life, that he may speak to us and we to him. O Christ, show us the way to the Father; show us thyself; and open our eyes that we may see the Father in thee.

———

Christ is the visible expression of the invisible God.

O Spirit of the living God, who hast revealed thyself to us in a Person, like us and yet so unlike us, sharing our humanity, yet rising far above and beyond it; save us from all specious talk about him, and idle theorizing, and help us to stand in his presence, awed, renewed, and forgiven as in the presence of thyself.

———

O Christ, who in human form didst reveal to us the mystery and the wonder of God, help us to keep close to thee, for we

27

need tangible things to lead us to the things that are intangible, and we need a way that we can see to lead us to the things that are eternal and invisible; help us to follow thee more nearly, and know thee more clearly, and love thee more dearly.

———

We thank thee, O God, for the life of Jesus, for the wonder of it, the power of it; the beauty and glory of it, the simplicity of it, the kindness and the compassion. Open our eyes that we may see that life wherever it expresses itself in our midst and, when we see it, give us the courage to believe once again that thou, in all thy majesty, art reigning over everything that we do or think or say.

———

I must be about my Father's business.

I must preach the kingdom of God.

I must go to Jerusalem and suffer many things.

O God, as we try to follow Jesus is these last days of his earthly life, give us the imagination to see him as he really was, and give us also the will to capture in ourselves something of the same spirit, that mature obedience by which the kingdom of heaven is opened to all who sincerely seek it. We ask this in the name of him who humbled himself and became a man and was obedient unto death, even the death of the cross.

———

O God and Master of us all, help us to put into practice in our daily lives these things that we believe and think so sincerely and so seriously; and as we go about our way, help us so to live that we may be more nearly measured by the character of our Lord and Master, Jesus Christ.

———

When things are dark and there is not much to look forward to, either in our own lives or in the life of the world, help us,

28

O God, to remember those who have hoped in Jesus. In him they found thee and in thee they found something that surpassed everything that this world can offer and, at the same time, make everything in this life shine with a new splendor.

———

The spirit indeed is willing but the flesh is weak.

Not the will, O God, do we lack, but the power to be like Jesus. Keep him so clearly before us as we go about our way day by day, and draw us so closely into his companionship that we may desire even more than we do now to be like him; and by the power of association may we grow more and more like him as we are more ready to recognize our shortcomings.

———

O God, who hast shown us the perfect life of Jesus, help us as we are drawn to that unattainable ideal. Save us from discouragement, and give us the strength and wisdom to go steadily on our way, cultivating the qualities we admire and reaching out for every sort of help that can come from thee and from him. We ask this because we love him and admire him and want to be like him.

———

And as Jesus went out of the temple, one of his disciples saith unto him, Master, see what manner of stones and what buildings are here.

O God, who in Jesus hath given us a clear vision of the nature of things, help us to correct our vision by his vision, and as we grow in age may we grow in discernment and discrimination, that knowing and seeing what things are important we may reach after those things in which we can find our own security and by which we can rise to the adequacy we so sincerely desire.

O God, who hast revealed thyself to us in Jesus our Lord and Master, help us to turn to him in simplicity, sincerity and truth that we may always be conscious of the highest possibilities as we find them in him, and let us never rest until we have come near him who is the Truth and the Way and the Life.

––––––––

O spirit of the living Christ, do thou overtake us on our way; reveal to us the meaning of the strange and perplexing events through which we must move; open our eyes to recognize thy presence in every form of life and love; and help us at the end of the way to understand afresh that the meaning of life is to be found in the breaking.

––––––––

Whosoever exalteth himself shall be abased; and he that humbleth himself shall be exalted.

As we try to understand ourselves, O God, bring us into closer and closer contact with thy Son Jesus Christ, our Master, that we, like him, may be so secure in thee that we may fear no enemy, and may be delivered from all false pride and ambition, and may go forward on our way through life, sensitive to other people, their feelings and their rights, not looking for the things that the world prizes, but finally finding the things that are real and true and good. We ask this, O God, in the name of Jesus.

––––––––

We acknowledge, O God, in ourselves the desire to seek our own way and to have our own will regardless of what it may cost us or other people. Open our eyes to these facts, unpleasant as they may be, and then interpret to us the teaching of thy church that we may be prepared to meet the crooked streak that runs through our world, and finally be saved from it, through Jesus Christ our Lord.

O God, who hast put into our hearts the desire to help and to heal those who are in trouble, grant that we may never pass by those serious situations which seem beyond our individual control. Unite us in great bodies of service by which the sore spots of the world by thine own power will be healed.

O God, who hast gathered thy people together in this house of worship and this place of prayer, grant that we may commit ourselves to thee and to thy purpose for us, and that we may go forth from this place, strengthened and renewed in body, mind and spirit, to do thy work and to let thy light shine through us into the world.

As we take the thorns of life and try to work them into some kind of pattern, O God, let us not waste our energies wondering about the trouble in the world, but use them to meet it; to take it away, if that be possible; but if it be not possible, give us the grace to take up our trouble like a cross, and bear it proudly in the name of Jesus our Lord.

Be ye perfect, even as your Father who is in heaven is perfect.

O God, we would not settle for low things, but reach for high things. Let not the disappointments that have hurt us lead into the temptation of thinking that we are not able to do the things that our Lord Jesus Christ has asked of us. When we hear his call, when we are aware of his confidence in us, give us the grace to respond, and do the best we can to care as much as we can for as many as we can.

Quicken our minds, O God, with the remembrance of the heroism of those who in old days went out and did great things, not thinking of themselves, not taking into account

31

the consequences. Give us a courage like theirs, so that into this world which is so near the brink of a great crisis, we may bring some of the life and the spirit of our Lord and Master.

––––––––

Give us, O God, the courage to do the things we talk about and to practice the faith we preach. Let us never withdraw into the cloister for our own safety, but let us be there long enough to find our true center in him who will give us strength to keep our eyes on the distant goal, and to navigate as well as we can.

––––––––

When we begin to be sorry for ourselves, O God, and try to escape the duties and burdens that accompany a good life, grant that we may see once again with a new freshness the life of Jesus, and seeing him, help us to go out not with straining effort but with a joyful and triumphant will to live in him. We want, O God, above everything else, to grow up into him who is the Way, the Truth, and the Life.

––––––––

Shake us out of our old habits and ruts and help us to think greater thoughts and see larger visions, O Lord, no matter how old we may be. But if we are young, don't let us waste these precious years. Draw us into the orbit of Christ wherever we find him. We ask it in the name of him who as a young man went out to save the world.

––––––––

O Christ, who brought into our dull, drab lives so much brightness and so great a glory, raise us to higher levels where we may in thy name and by thy power go out and turn the desert into a flowering place and make the lives of men and women leap for joy because of thee.

HOLY SPIRIT AND HIS GIFTS

. . . filled with the Holy Spirit . . .

O Spirit of the Living God, who hast filled this place in times past, fill it now again that the people who come here may be strengthened and renewed to do thy will, enabled to surpass themselves and to share and show that love which belongs only to thee, the love of the perfect Father of all the children.

———————

I am come that they might have life, and that they might have it more abundantly.

Guide us, O God, through the mysterious ways of life. Save us from thinking that we can storm the gates of life, and pick for ourselves its fruit. Give us rather the tranquil spirit of waiting and watching, that we may go about our ways quietly, so that when the great experiences of life come we may be ready to receive and enjoy them, through Jesus Christ our Lord.

———————

Give us, O God, the spirit which will enable us to hold passionate convictions and yet exercise dispassionate judgments. Give us more tolerance and less temper. Help us to see both sides of a question, and as we face the complicated issues of our day, fill us with that spirit which will enable us to stand for the right and the truth, without bitterness and without any loss of loving-kindness.

———————

In the midst of our confusion, O God, show us thy way. When we try the high way and meet defeat, save us from despair and bitter disappointment. Give us the grace to take the lower road in such a way that other people traveling it will be lifted up to heights hitherto unknown. We remember in all these things how Jesus went the high way, first through life and then through death.

We ask, O God, for the strength and the help to meet whatever opposition comes to us in life with determination and patience, trusting not in violence or force, but in the things of the spirit by which those conquer who are willing to suffer if need be, and to die, and live again.

———

Lift up your eyes on high and see.

O God, who hast given to us the wonderful and mysterious gift of sight, help us to open our eyes that we may see the world that lies around us; help us to see not only the unpleasant things but the beautiful and good things that fill our world, and then give us that deeper sight by which we may see thyself.

———

There is nothing hidden that shall not be revealed.

Open the eyes of our understanding, O God, to the things that we can see, and gird up our loins to discover and find the things which are hidden. Keep us humble in all our ways, and yet high in all our thoughts and amibitions, that we may live a life that is worthy of the possibilities which thou hast prepared for those that love thee.

———

He withdrew himself into the wilderness, and prayed.

Teach us, O God, how to withdraw from the pressures of life, not in self-interest or self-indulgence, but to find the quietness and the strength that we need in order that we may handle life and handle it well. Help us to remember Jesus, and how in his withdrawing and returning, he fulfilled one of thy laws and made his life great and rich for all others.

———

I will say of the Lord, he is my refuge and my fortress: my God, in him will I trust.

We know, O God, that everything we are and have, and everything that we can ever hope to be, ultimately comes from thee. Keep alive in us that sense of dependence upon thee, and give us the grace and the wisdom so to cooperate with thy laws that we may work together with thee to do things which by ourselves we could never accomplish at all.

———

Lord, if it be thou, bid me come unto thee on the water. And Jesus said, Come.

O God, give us the will and the desire to launch out into deep waters, and to aim for the goals that are high and difficult; make us responsive to great things when they call us; when our own powers are inadequate, show us where to turn for the help we need. These things we ask in trust and confidence in the name of Jesus Christ our Lord.

———

Isaac loved Esau, because he ate of his game; but Rebekah loved Jacob.

O God, our life is spoiled so many times by antagonisms that poison and corrupt it. Help us whenever it is possible to moderate them, to understand the differences that may separate us from other people, to appreciate their lives as well as our own, and over and above it all, help us to see thee, who art guiding us through these struggles; may we be in the channel of thy purpose for us and for humanity, not with the biggest, but with the best and the wisest.

———

Jesus, moved with compassion . . .

O Christ, who came among us to care for all sorts and conditions of men, help us to control our dislike of other people and lead us further along the way of compassion. Take us in hand when we begin to grow callous and make us like thee, who didst reach out to all men with the love of God.

———

O God, open our eyes to see the things that are happening around us. Quicken our minds and hearts to interpret what

35

we see so that, as thou art trying to speak to us, we will always be ready to listen. Help us to find our way, though we sometimes are strangers in very strange places, knowing that wherever we are, we are always at home in thee.

————

Help us, O God, to express the gratitude and appreciation which we feel deeply in our hearts. Spare us from carelessness and shallowness, and help us to remember always what it means to another person and to thee when we put into words how we feel. Bless us as we go about our work in thy name and on behalf of thy church, and to thy name be the power and the glory.

————

Open our hearts, O Lord, that we may love those who do not love us; help us to restrain our natural tendency to resent the wrongs that people do to us and to take offense easily and quickly, and to nurse tenderly our grievances and grudges. May this day bring a new love into our lives and may we be purified by that love as we move on into the future.

————

As we become aware, O God, of our deepest needs and our inability to meet them by ourselves, give us the courage as well as the humility to reach out to thine infinite resources. Make us not ashamed or afraid to cry to thee, our Father, and to ask for the things which we sincerely desire, knowing that thou canst not always give them to us, and wishing above all things that thy will may be done, not ours.

————

As we direct our thoughts to the great problems of life, help us, O God, to think clearly, and then lead us out of ourselves toward him who is the purpose of all men, that we may show forth in our lives something of his life, that the world through us may be reconciled to thee.

We thank thee, O God, for the ideals and standards by which we try to live, and for the ordered way of life in the faithful fellowship of thy church. Grant that we may never be so immersed in that way of life that we become immune to the life of those who are groping their way through the shadows and thick darkness, trying to find happiness and freedom. Help us to remember him who came not to call the righteous but the sinner into his kingdom.

Open the eyes of our understanding, O God, as we try to interpret thy word to us. Keep our minds clear, our imaginations alive, and our hearts pure and humble, that we may turn to the great Book in which we find thy Word, knowing that in it thou wilt somehow speak to us and to our condition.

We thank thee, O God, for the joy that has come into our lives through Christ Jesus. May we never forget that religion without that joy is not his religion; and as we live and grow in it, may we not forget that ours is the privilege of taking that joy into the lives of other people. We ask this in the spirit and in the name of him who came to turn the water of life into wine.

Lead us, O Lord, out of our little lives into the greater world of service and understanding and enjoyment. May we never be satisfied with ourselves, and always reach for the things that are beyond our grasp. We ask these things in the name of him who as Love came among us, Jesus Christ our Lord.

Open our minds and hearts, O God, to the mystery of thy truth. May we not shrink from the fact of reckoning in our lives. Make us generous in our judgment of others and, while we continue to maintain order in thy church, may we never keep out anyone who is looking for thee, no matter how they may appear to us at the moment. We ask these things in the spirit and in the name and power of Jesus Christ our Lord.

––––––––

O God, we reach out for the joy that is not to be found in the chances and changes of the world, but in thee. Open our eyes that we may see every sign of thy life and love moving and working among us. And raise us up that we may help others to rise, for only as we become the instruments of thy love will our gladness be unconquerable.

––––––––

Lord, as we face the facts and riddles of existence, we are often honestly disturbed and perplexed. Help us to be our real selves always. Let us never be content with ourselves as we are, but move ever onward to a greater and deeper understanding to thy truth. Help us to rest so firmly on the things that we do believe, that the things that are still in shadow may finally be made real and clear to us. We ask this in the name of Jesus.

––––––––

We thank thee, O God, for our Church. We love it and find in it the things that satisfy our deepest desires and our most urgent necessities. Help us, O God, to see how other men have found other ways, and while we may never overlook the real differences that divide us, help us to grow in understanding of those who are different from us. And above all, O God, keep us humble, through Christ our Lord.

––––––––

O God, who hast set before us so many and such great choices, thou knowest that we are divided often in our own hearts and that we do not know which way to go. Help us to remember that there are some things that are wrong and that the responsibility for what we do ultimately rests upon ourselves. Give us that awareness of right and wrong that will save us from our final folly, through him who made another weep, even Jesus our Lord.

PART ·II·

PRAYERS
FOR SPECIAL
NEEDS

Prayers for Special Needs

For the Ability to Care:

O God, who hast set before us an ideal that is far beyond our reach, but who hast also promised to give us the power we need to come closer to it, increase our capacity to care for other people. We have no other reason for being here. O God, bring this to pass in us this day.

———

O God, take that buried impulse to care for other people and make it grow until we care more and more about more and more people; until through us thine own care is made real and thine own arms support those who are falling.

For Right Judgment:

Help us, O God, to make right judgments in difficult situations. Grant that we may never spare ourselves or our own

41

feelings. Help us always to be kind no matter what the circumstances may be; give us the courage to be honest, and the grace and confidence to be humble, that in all things we may show forth the spirit of him who came among us, Jesus, Our Lord.

––––––––

O God, give us the courage to say what we mean and mean what we say, to know when to tell the whole truth and nothing but the truth, and when to hold back some of the truth in order to save another person's heartache. Help us to distinguish between love and truth and see how they go together and how they stand apart. And send us leaders, O God, who are willing to say what they mean and mean what they say.

––––––––

Show me the way, O God, that I cannot find for myself. Help me to see how this man looks to you, and put out of my mind how he seems to me. Keep me on the right track, and let not my self-pity throw me off. I want more than anything to keep my relationship with people direct, warm, and steady. I know that I cannot always do it; I know that I have not always done it. But help me this time to know what is right and give me the power to do it.

For Tolerance:

Help us, O God, as we try to find our way, especially in relation to those who differ from us, those who are opposed to us. Keep our eyes always on the new dimension of love as it was revealed and incarnate in Jesus, and may we never be satisfied with ourselves until we have done everything we can to rise from the level of the selfish life we live to the higher level of love where we are with him, and he is with us.

––––––––

Open our minds, O God, to the truth that never changes, and help us to be flexible in our own minds and hearts, and ready to change our ways of living and thinking when we come to see clearly that something revealed to us in our own time is true and right and good.

————

O God, our life is spoiled so many times by antagonisms that poison and corrupt it; help us whenever it is possible to moderate them; help us to understand the differences that may separate us from other people, to appreciate their lives as well as our own, and then over and above it all, help us to see thee, who art guiding us through these struggles; may we be in the channel of thy purpose for us and for humanity, not with the biggest, but with the best and the wisest.

————

Lead us, O Lord, through the difficult and crooked ways of our world. Help us to make wise decisions; save us from our prejudices, and give us the grace to listen to people who differ from us, if we can see that they are sincere and honest in what they want, in what they think. Bind us together in one great family with many different opinions and many different ways of life, and unite us in our effort to show men in some specific way the compassion that was once in Christ Jesus.

For Guidance:

O God, guide us through the dark places in life. Grant that we may not fear the loss of thee, knowing that thou art always by our side, and that life will renew itself in us if we give it time and are willing to wait. And as we rise out of the low places through which we sometimes must walk, help us to be thankful for them, because through them and by them we may be able to help someone else through the darkness into light.

————

O God, who dost often lead us by way of the wilderness toward uncertain difficulties and futures of which we cannot be sure, help us to trust always in thy guiding purpose and in the plan that rules our lives and, when we are fearful and inclined to go back, give us the courage to stand still and then to go forward knowing that the strength we need is the strength we will be given.

———————

O God, when we feel helpless in situations that look hopeless, give us the honesty to say what we feel and think, and then lead us to the place where we will find strength; guide us to thyself as thou hast made thyself known to us in Christ Jesus: and in him who is both power and love may we find the strength we need to live our lives in the spirit of him who is our Lord.

———————

O God, open our ears that we listen carefully to him who is the truth, the way, and the life. Give us those critical faculties which prevent our being deceived by our own reasoning powers. If we are wrong in thinking that he is saying something to us that he is not saying, show us, O God, what it is. And when we know what he says, help us to take it in and follow it.

———————

As we go on our way with the winds often against us, help us, O God, to trust and believe in the best we know, to do the best we can, and to be the best we are. Save us from all cheap and easy explanations, and lead us more and more into the deep understanding of the truth that is in Christ Jesus, thy Son, our Lord and our God.

For Growth:

O God, who art clothed in mystery as well as majesty, teach us to approach thy presence with reverence and awe; prepare us

44

for the fact that all our questions will never be answered and that the way to thee, as to all the great things in life, is not an easy way. Then speak to us in all the things that mean most to us, in the wonders of the physical world, in its knowability and intelligibility, in our need for thee and in our response to thy law, that we may grow in thee and for thee, now and always.

For Honesty:

In our prayers, O God, draw us closer to thyself; help us always to be honest and real, to say no more than we really think and really want, and yet keep us always reaching outward and upward to a more perfect image of thyself, until at last we are joined with Jesus our Lord, so that with him on his cross we know that only the infinite pity is sufficient for the infinite pathos of human life.

A Parent's Prayer:

Help us, O God, in the relationships of life, to let those we love live their own lives, and to love them when we can no longer understand them. Help us to trust them, and to trust thee, and then so open our hearts and minds that Christ Jesus may bring into them something of the greatness of his life and love. We ask these things in his name.

For the Middle Years:

O God, as we face the middle years of life, with their disappointments and regrets, and lack of fulfillment, help us to look for the things that are so great that they demand all that we have and are. Grant that we may cease to think of the things that we can keep, and begin to think more constantly of the things that we can give. Help us to give ourselves to something great, that we may lose ourselves and so find ourselves, for it is only in losing our lives that we can ever hope to find them.

For Unselfishness in Prayer:

Keep my prayers from being too selfish, Lord. Turn my mind first toward thyself and let me remember thy love before I rehearse my needs. The steady movement of the earth gives us a glimpse of thy dependable care, but the ways of the storm we do not understand, and destruction is hard for us to comprehend. Help us to remember that love is too deep for us to measure and too mysterious for us to know completely. We can receive it and we can give it. Help us to do both.

In Preparation For Worship:

God is spirit, and they that worship him must worship him in spirit and in truth.

Never let the way we worship thee, O Lord, be more important to us than the spirit in which we do it; and never let us be so tied to our local ways that we forget that other people have other ways.

Deliver us, dear Lord, from smallness when we worship thee, and swallow up our pettiness in the grandeur of thy spirit and truth.

———

Let us be still, and remember Jesus as he was then, powerful to heal, to speak, to save. Think of him as he is now, powerful as the Spirit of God among us, to lift us up out of the low places and set our feet once again on the high way. O God, draw us to him who is the perfect incarnation of thyself, that our power may more and more be tamed by the power of his love.

For Strength:

When the disciples were alone with Jesus, the first question they asked him was, Why couldn't we do it?

We are conscious, O God, of our spiritual weakness. Help us to renew those energies which we need if we are to drive out the devils of our world. Help us to take time apart from the world of busy activity, and ground us in the things that we really believe so that when Jesus lifts us up, we shall be able to stand on our own feet.

For Standing for What Is Right:

Open our eyes, O God, to all the facts of life; give us the strength to face it with courage, not shrinking from the evil, but always striving for that which is right and true and good, knowing that we are sons of thine, and that in all things, thy love and thy power will be made known through us.

O God, we are thankful for every quiet voice that raises itself against the opposition of the majority, not in anger, not in stormy protest, but simply and quietly, saying the thing it believes, doing the thing that it knows to be right.

For Resisting Evil:

Help us, O God, when we are likely to go astray; teach us how to discipline and train our desires; save us from blindness to our own sins, and in the light of the glory of Christ, reveal to us ourselves as we really are, so that from thence we can proceed until we become new creatures, through Christ our Lord.

Help us, O God, as we fight against those things which hold us back from the goal. Purify our lives, clarify our thinking and strengthen our wills, that as we love him who loved us we may grow to be more like him.

In Difficult Times:

Open our eyes, O God, that we see not only the beauty but also the ugliness of the world, not only the good but the evil; and then take away our discouragement and give us that fortitude of spirit that will send us with Jesus as he went out into the night when he was betrayed to take up his cross for the good of mankind.

O God, when the winds are against us, help us to keep our spirits and our wills and our minds serene and strong; we know that all things are not arranged for our comfort and our convenience; we know that there will be times when things will go against us; but we know, too, that thou hast given us the spirit whereby we may be the master of our lives; help us so to put our trust in thee that though the winds be against us, we will go steadily on our way.

Guide us, O God, through these difficult ways; help us to think straight, to love more generously, to live more nobly; give us the courage to take greater risks in the name of great things, as we strive to be the worthy servants of thy Son Jesus Christ, our Lord.

O thou who art beyond and yet within the stream of events which so quickly rushes by, open our eyes that we may see thee. If we cannot see thee, tell us that there are others who do, so that we may be steadied and prepared to meet whatever happens to us without panic, knowing that within this stream of life, thou art always present, and always ready to help.

On the Unfairness of Life:

When the pressures of life exceed our power to meet them, save us, O God, from thinking that the end has come; spare us from the bitterness which comes to many when they find life hard and unfair. Open our eyes to see thy presence in the time of trouble so that we may see it at all times and in all places, and that we may live knowing that we live not by ourselves, but by the strength that thou hast given us.

On Losing Our Way:

O Keeper of Sheep, I have the will but not always the power to follow. When I go astray, look for me and find me. Take me back where I belong and set me up on the right way again. At the end, lead me to my Father's house and leave me in His care.

O thou who art the incarnation of meaning, help us to find our way when we begin to wonder whether life has any meaning at all. At those moments stand thou before us, O Christ, in the appearance of a man. Point us to the things that we have missed; draw us to thyself; and then lead us outward into the mystery and the wonder of God's love.

Remember, O God, those who are now losing their way in life; be thou their pole star; remind them of thy searching care surrounding them always and, as they look for thee, bring them back into the haven where they long to be.

O God, in times of dryness when nothing seems to happen and we wonder whether we are worth anything at all, remind us of Jesus in the barren, bleak places of the wilderness. Let us not forget that he will help us through our conflicts to move through the wilderness out into the light where there is hope, and joy, and confidence, and faith.

For Controlling Our Tempers:

O God, help us to grow in love. Help us to control our tempers when they get out of hand, to think twice before we speak, to remember that the person we are speaking to is our brother. And help us to love more and more, because thy love is in us and overflows toward other people.

––––––

Fill us, O Christ, with thy Spirit. Take the raw material of our lives and refine it. Cool our tempers, soften our speech, enlarge our understanding, deepen our love. When the test comes, we will trust in thee and not in ourselves, knowing that by thy Spirit we will be able to do all things.

On Holding Grudges:

O God, open our hearts and minds to thy love as we see it revealed in Jesus. Knowing all our difficulties and our selfishness, help us to press toward the mark that he set for us, to harbor no bitterness in our lives, to keep no grudge at the center of our hearts and more and more to show forth in imitation of him the love which alone can conquer evil.

On Gossiping:

O God, give us such a vision of truth that we may have no patience with idle tales and careless gossip which hurt people and make their chances of life less sure than they otherwise would be. Help us in all our dealings with other people to be honest and trustworthy ourselves and give us that deep respect and regard for people as people which we find in Jesus our Lord and Saviour.

When We Make Mistakes:

We thank thee, O God, for the love that was in Christ Jesus; for his never-failing care for the people who had made mistakes; for his willingness to live with them and die for them. In his love we feel the love that will not let us go, and with him we are bound together in thy family.

O God, give us the courage to face the stern facts of life, knowing that behind them thou art there, to judge, to understand, to love, to redeem. No matter how many mistakes we make, we always have another chance. Give us the grace to acknowledge our mistakes and the courage to rise up to take another chance.

Thanks be to thee, O God, for the life that is in Jesus, and for the light that comes to us from him and guides us on our way and makes sense of life, that gives us a better direction. Steady us, O Lord, for the way we have to go. Save us from unnecessary mistakes; and when we make them, help us to remember that thou art not only our Judge, but also our Father.

For Serving Others:

Take our lives, O God, and lift them up, not into prominence, but into places where their power may be mobilized for thy sake. Help us to see the opportunities which thou hast given us to continue the ministry of Jesus in the world, and then give us the will and the grace to do it, knowing that we are sent into this world where there is trouble and distress and sorrow and sin, to bring something of his light and love into the valleys of the shadow of darkness.

O God, we would not settle for low things, but reach for high things. Let not the disappointments that have hurt us lead us into the temptation of thinking that we are not able to do the things that our Lord Jesus Christ has asked of us. When we hear his call, when we are aware of his confidence in us, give us the grace to respond, and do the best we can to care as much as we can for as many as we can.

Lord speak to us that we may speak. Tell us where to go and what to do; open our ears to hear the message, and give us the will to do what we are told. May we never be too proud to play the minor part, or too preoccupied with ourselves to get up and go wherever and to whomsoever thou dost send us.

For a Daring Faith:

O God, who hast taught us to trust in thee as our loving Father, open our hearts and share that most daring faith which thou hast revealed to thy servants in all ages, till the littleness of our knowledge is lost in the greatness of thy love.

PRAYERS FOR SPECIAL TIMES

In Changing Times:

Guide us, O God, as we move through troubled waters. Save us, above everything else, from self-righteousness. Keep our minds open and alert, knowing that life is always changing and that we must be ready for change; and give us the anchors that we need to hold us to the things that are real and true and good. We ask this in the name of Jesus our Lord and Master.

We live, O God, in a world that is forever changing. Give us such power of discernment that we may distinguish that which changes for the better from that which changes for the worse. Then help us to see the things which do not change, and give us the courage to stand up for them, to speak out for them, and to live by them in our daily lives. We ask all these things in the name of Jesus, the same yesterday, today and forever.

In Uncertainty:

Fear not, stand still, and see the salvation of the Lord.

And the children of Israel walked upon the dry land in the midst of the sea.

O God, who dost often lead us by way of the wilderness toward uncertain difficulties and futures of which we cannot be sure, help us to trust always in thy guiding purpose and in the plan that rules our lives. When we are fearful and inclined to go back, give us the courage to stand still and then go forward knowing that the strength we need is the strength we will be given.

In Time of Trouble:

Our lives are not always easy, O God, and we ask for strength to meet the difficult things that the days may bring to us. Open our eyes to the shining things that lie ahead of us. Help us to put the past behind us, and pour all our energies into the race that lies before us, keeping our eyes always steadfastly on him who is the Way, the Truth, and the Life.

Help us, O God, as we are overtaken by dangers and difficulties that are too deep for our understanding; grant that we may have no fear, and that putting our trust not in ourselves but in thy power and thy love we may go forward to new victories through him who saved us, Jesus Christ, our Lord.

———————

O God, help us to be still now, to set aside all the tensions, the normal responsibilities and exertions of the working day, and rest in thee as though we were held in the everlasting arms. Teach us to go gladly on our way for the sake of those we love, and when our burdens are too heavy to bear give us the grace to ask for help from thee.

In Loneliness:

O God, help me to get along without people and to find things to do and think about, when there are no people to talk to. I have many resources within myself and there are many things that I can and should do. Give me, O Lord, the will to do them. Let me not stand still, except when I am waiting for thee, and may I not idly waste the precious hours which once passed are gone forever. I see the riches all around me; take my eyes off everything else, that I be not misled by lesser things; and then put me in action, Lord; quiet, steady action, that I myself may richer be.

In Discouragement:

O God, take the shortages of our lives and the few things that we have and multiply them until they are adequate to our need and to thy purpose. Let us never become discouraged because we have too little; remind us always how Christ took the little that people had and made it more than meet for five thousand.

In Failure:

O God, open our eyes to the stern fact that there is a chance of failure in our life, and help us to see the vision of him who is our Lord and Master. Let him lift us out of the low ways of failure and lead us on toward a life which, in spite of failures, will in some measure catch the spirit of his greatness.

———

As we follow at so great a distance in the steps of him who is our Lord, our Master, our Guide, grant, O God, that we may never be discouraged by our failures but still reach out toward him who is far beyond us, and bring into our world some small fragment of his tenderness, his strength, his clarity, and his judgment.

In Temptation:

O God, who hast taught us to trust and love thee, as children trust and love their parents, help us when we are tempted to go our own way and pay no mind to the call that we hear from thee. We know that thou dost understand our temptations and our weaknesses, and all that thou askest of us is trust and love. Save us from the danger of disobedience, O God, that our lives may not fail.

In Anxiety:

The weather may be better or worse, we cannot tell. If it gets worse, help us to remember, O Lord, that it always changes, and that the dark skies hide a sun that is still bright. If it gets better, let its brightness not blind us to thy goodness; and in our gladness let us not forget thee, whose goodness is the source of all our joy.

About Fears:

Cleanse thou me, O God, from my secret fears. Help me to search them out and know them. But they are buried too deep for me; I cannot reach them. Thou alone canst touch them and take them away. As the wind ceased when thou didst step into the boat beside thy friends who were afraid, come now and calm the troubled waters of my life. And if this be not thy will, and if my fears cannot be taken away, help me to take them quietly, and in them find a deeper faith.

For a Dark Day:

When the day is dark and I am right at
    home, with no desire to go anywhere or
    do anything,
Then pick me up, Lord, and carry me
    through.

There have been many other days like this,
    and always someone has come from some-
    where, or something has happened some-
    how, and I have come through.
In appearance strange and unfamiliar, Jesus
    himself drew near and went with me.

    Lord, help me to remember how the fog
    lifted when he made himself known.

In Sickness:

Young woman, your faith has cured you.

O God, we thank thee for our bodies, and for the power that thou dost give us to keep and make them well. Give us a realistic faith in thy power and goodness, and when we go through the valley of suffering and sickness, help us to trust in thy loving care and power.

In Time of Suffering:

Perplexed as we are, O God, by the suffering we cannot understand, let us never be paralyzed or defeated by it. Hold thou the cross before our eyes, and help us to find in it both the power and the grace to take whatever life brings us and use it in such a way that it will make life better for other people.

In Bereavement:

Give us the strength, O God, to meet life from day to day victoriously; to approach the things that are difficult without fear; to keep our spirits quiet and serene and our hearts brave, and finally as we see those we love come to the end of their way, may we triumph over death as well as over life; in the name and by the power of him who took his thorns and wore them as a crown.

On Prayer:

O God, who art the source of every good thing in our lives, when we pray, help us to remember that all that we have, or ever hope to be, comes from thee. And then give us the grace to ask for the things that we want most, leaving it to thy judgment and thy goodness, to grant them or to withhold them. Teach us, Lord Jesus, in this hard world of mechanism and impersonal enterprise, to pray and to pray wisely and humbly.

On Friendship:

We thank Thee, O God, for our friends, men and women, old and young, who have stood by us and understood us, shared our sorrows and our joys; give us the grace to be a friend, to go out to others, to help them in their time of trouble, and when the time comes that all friends fail, help us then to rest in thee, our great Companion who never fails.

On the Influence of Other Lives:

O God, we live in a confused and troubled world. Sometimes the Christ we follow is completely hidden from us. Help us to see him in the lives of other people who but dimly reflect his presence, and may we never fail to reach out to him who reaches out to us.

———

We thank thee, O God, for those men and women who have been channels of thy power and strength. As we turn to them now release in us the strength they once gave to others, that in these days of stress and strain we may have in some small degree the vitality and the life that they had in such abundance. We ask this in the name of him who is the Life, and whose life is given for us all, Jesus Christ.

———

We thank thee, O God, for all the people in our lives through whom thy power and love and strength have come to us; open our eyes to the fact that when we need help there is always help available; take away our pride and our suspicions and our fears until we stand before thee in all our naked reality, waiting only upon thee, knowing that in some human shape our help will finally come to us, through Jesus Christ our Lord.

———

We thank thee, O God, for those who have brought thee near to us, and led us into thy presence. Give us a portion of that humility which the great always have and help us through them to be more and more conscious of thy love and power.

On Holiday:

Open my arms, O Lord, to what lies ahead and rouse my sluggish spirit to respond to whatever it may be. Renew the fearless anticipation of earlier days and keep me from getting too well set in my ways. There is so much to know, so many things to do, so many worlds still untouched, do not let me fold my hands and stay where I am. Keep me open, Lord — my eyes, my ears, and my mind open to what is all around me, that I may not miss thy glory or thy goodness, wherever they may be and however they may appear.

On War:

O Christ, give us the wisdom to choose wisely and the strength to carry out our choices; help us to stand fast when we have made a right choice, not to be swayed by the opinion of others or by our own convenience and give to the nations of the world the imagination and the will to reject once and for all war and the weapons of war. We ask this in the name of Jesus.

———————

O God, we pray for our country and our world. We ask for protection, but even more for guidance; for knowledge, but even more for imagination; for power, but even more for grace; to do and be the kind of people who change the climate and avert the storm before it starts.

In Quietness:

Let us turn once again to the things that are true and beautiful and good, not to escape the issues of our day, but to fortify us to meet them well. Deepen our roots, O God, that we may stand steady as a tree in a storm.

In the Hospital:

Master my impatience, Lord;
Muzzle my fears, and stretch my faith to
    match my need.
Take me off my mind, and fill my thoughts
    with other people's pain far worse than
    mine.
Devour my smallness, Lord, and grow me
    to my stature full, my height, my breadth,
    and depth.
That I may meet what comes and make it
    mine;
That I may more and more be thine.

———————

This is another day. I know not what it
    will bring forth, but make me ready,
    Lord, for whatever it may be.
If I am to stand up, help me to stand
    bravely.
If I am to sit still, help me to sit quietly.
If I am to lie low, help me to do it pa-
    tiently.
And if I am to do nothing, let me do it gal-
    lantly.
Make these words more than words, and
    give me the Spirit of Jesus.

———————

Help me, Lord, to keep my discouragements
    to myself;
Let me not dim the brightness of anybody
    else's day;

Let no gloom of mine be added to the
    shadows through which the people
    around me already grope.
And what I keep to myself, let me finally
    cast upon thee, O Lord, and lose my
    darkness in thy Light.

––––––––

Through the lives of others thy healing power streams. Keep
them going, O Lord, through thick and thin, strain and
stress; and may we who wait for them add nothing unnecessary to their work. When they are weary at the end of
the day, give them the blessing of satisfaction and the
renewal of complete rest.

––––––––

When I begin to feel better, Lord, let me
    not forget thee.
If I turn to thee when I am in trouble, how
    much more shall I turn to thee when I
    am not in trouble!
To thank thee for all my health, and for
    the prospect of brighter days ahead;
To ask thee for the good sense to enjoy
    my health, but not to waste it;
To offer thee my body, my will, my mind.

––––––––

Shut up in this little room, surrounded by these four bare
walls, keep me, O Lord, from feeling cut off from life. The
air I breathe and the light by which I see are signs of the
world outside. The kindness that surrounds me and the care
that never lets me go are tokens of a world too big to crowd
me and too good to blot me out.

DEATH AND LIFE EVERLASTING

For Christian Perspective:

Let not the beauty of the world be hidden, O God, by the passing clouds of ugliness; and let not the goodness of which men are capable be obscured by the evil of which they are often the unconscious instruments. Keep our eyes open to the beauty that is always present, and blind us not to the ugliness which always threatens to spoil it. May we be continually prepared to see the goodness that is in man, and at the same time be not unmindful of the evil into which he so easily slips. We ask these things in remembrance of him who had the eyes to see both the goodness and the meanness of man.

———

O God, as we face the solemn wonder and mystery of death, which sooner or later comes to all of us, open our eyes to see it as part of the normal experience of life. Our departure is in thy hands, even as our birth was. Take away our fear of it; help us to welcome it when it comes, knowing that in it and behind it is thy goodness and thy greatness, and that no matter what happens we rest in thy care. We ask this in the name of Jesus our Lord.

At the Approach of Death:

O God, who in the arms of death dost gather all thy children unto thyself, let us not linger when the evening comes or, for fear of darkness, fail to trust thy love and care. As in the day and in the night thou art ever by our side, so in life and in death thou shalt keep us safe as in our Father's house.

———

O God, who art the Lord of Death as well as Life, help us to face these mysteries unafraid, in the assurance and confidence that comes to us from our Lord Jesus Christ, knowing that wherever he is, we will be also.

———

O God, we know that all things work together for good to them that love thee; we know that though we walk through the valley of the shadow of death, thou art always with us, and that there is nothing to fear but the loss of thee; we know that nothing can separate us from those we love, and that in thy safe keeping they are free from danger and harm.

Knowing these things, O God, may we go quietly forward from day to day, not looking too far ahead, taking each step with the confidence that what we are asked to do or bear, for that thou wilt give us the strength we need.